3377

17 JAZZ DUETS for Two Flutes

MUSIC MINUS ONE

Music Minus One

3377

CONTENTS

ISBN 1-59615-736-4

1. Togetherness

2. Jazzed Up Strauss

6 beats (2 measures) precede music.

Fast waltz ♩=168

3. Drawing Room Music With A Beat

6 beats (2 measures) precede music.

4. More Big Band

8 beats (2 measures) precede music.

5. For When Your Wife
Gets Tired Of All That Jazz

6. Pretty Music

5 beats (1 ¼ measure) precede music.
(1 2 3 4 / 1)

Slow ballad ♩=76

7. For Sheep Herders Only

4 beats (1 1/3 measure) precede music.

Slow waltz ♩=96

8. Chamber Music 1968

6 beats (2 measures) precede music.

Fast waltz ♩=152

9. Music To Get Your Jollies By

8 beats (2 measures) precede music.

Fast ♩=144

10. A Psychedelic Trip

4 taps (1 measure) precede music.

Slow ♩=80

11. Chinatown After Hours

12. For Lovers

13. Gypsy

4 beats (1 measure) precede music.

♩=100

14. Harmonic / Rhythmic Study

8 beats (2 measures) precede music.

15. Torchy

8 beats (2 measures) precede music.

Introduction

16. Triplet Study

8 beats (2 measures) precede music.

17. Just For Swinging

8 beats (2 measures) precede music.

Engraving: Wieslaw Novak

MUSIC MINUS ONE
50 Executive Boulevard
Elmsford, New York 10523-1325
800-669-7464 (U.S.)/914-592-1188 (International)

www.musicminusone.com
e-mail: mmogroup@musicminusone.com